HOW TO DRAW
CATS AND KITTENS

Written and Illustrated by
Frank C. Smith

SCHOLASTIC INC.
New York Toronto London Auckland Sydney

ISBN 0-590-44000-4

12 11 10   3 4 5/9

Printed in the U.S.A.   34

BELOW ARE THE BASIC SHAPES YOU'LL BE USING IN DRAWING CATS AND KITTENS.

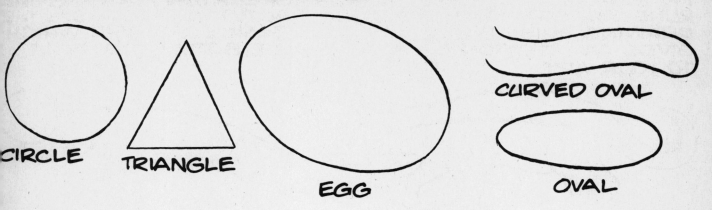

CIRCLE   TRIANGLE   EGG   CURVED OVAL   OVAL

THESE SHAPES ARE ONE DIMENSIONAL OR FLAT.

BELOW ARE THE SAME SHAPES DRAWN TWO DIMENSIONAL.

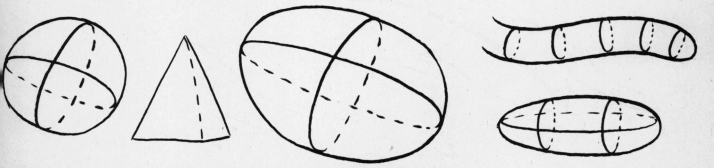

USE THESE SHAPES TO BUILD THE BODY OF A CAT. NOTICE THE PLACEMENT OF THE SHAPES IN THE DRAWING BELOW.

AN ACTION LINE IS AN
IMAGINARY LINE THAT
RUNS THROUGH YOUR
DRAWING. THIS LINE
GIVES A DIRECTION
TO YOUR ART.

THE STICK FIGURE OR
SKELETON FOLLOWS THE
ACTION LINE. THIS IS THE
BASIC STEP OVER WHICH
THE BODY IS DRAWN.

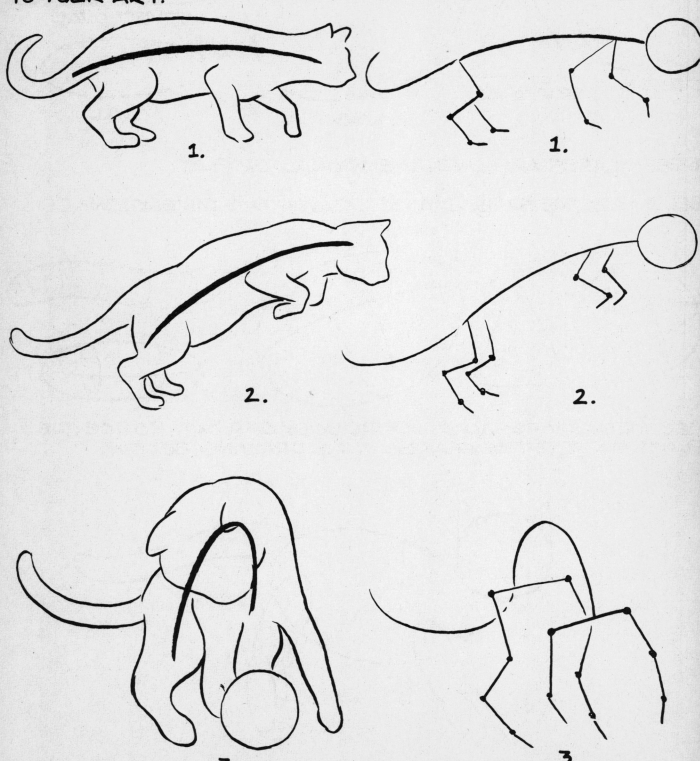

1.

1.

2.

2.

3.

3.

COMPARE THE DRAWINGS ON THE LEFT WITH THE SHAPES AT THE RIGHT. SOMETIMES IT HELPS TO STUDY A COMPLETED SKETCH OF WHAT YOU WANT TO DRAW. TRY TO VISUALIZE THE SHAPES IN THE CATS BODY ON THE LEFT.

START WITH A STICK FIGURE.

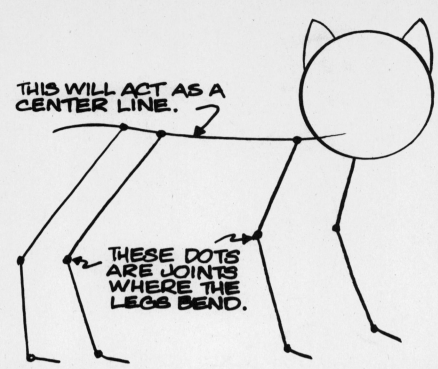

THIS WILL ACT AS A CENTER LINE.

THESE DOTS ARE JOINTS WHERE THE LEGS BEND.

THESE LINES ARE DRAWN LIGHTLY BECAUSE YOU WILL ERASE THEM IN THE FINISHED DRAWING.

LET'S LOOK AT THE PROPORTIONS OF A CAT.

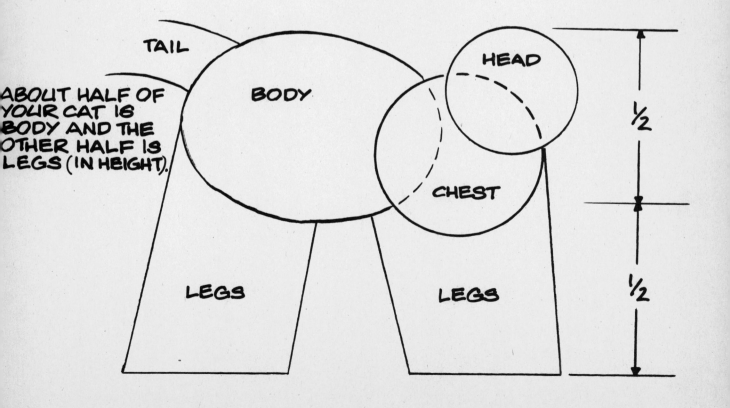

TAIL

ABOUT HALF OF YOUR CAT IS BODY AND THE OTHER HALF IS LEGS (IN HEIGHT).

BODY

HEAD

CHEST

½

LEGS   LEGS

½

WITH THE STICK FIGURE
DRAWN WE CAN NOW
START TO PUT THE BODY
OVER IT USING THE
BASIC SHAPES.

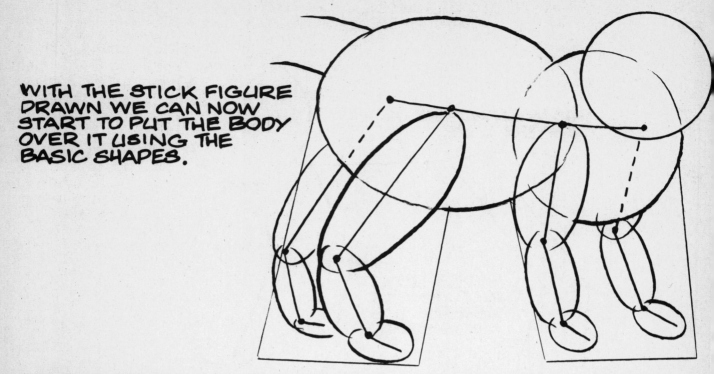

ON PAGE THREE WE TALKED ABOUT ADDING DIMENSION TO
THE DRAWINGS. THESE CENTER LINES WILL HELP IN THE
FINISH AND HELP TO POSITION EYES, NOSE, EARS AND LEGS.

CENTER
LINES

POSITIONING THE EYES, NOSE, SNOUT, ETC., CAN BE EASY IF YOU FOLLOW THESE SIMPLE RULES.

EYES ARE PLACED BELOW THE CENTER LINE.

IMAGINE AN OVAL THE SAME SIZE AS THE EYES, IN THE CENTER OF THE HEAD, AND YOU CAN SEE WHERE TO PLACE THE EYES.

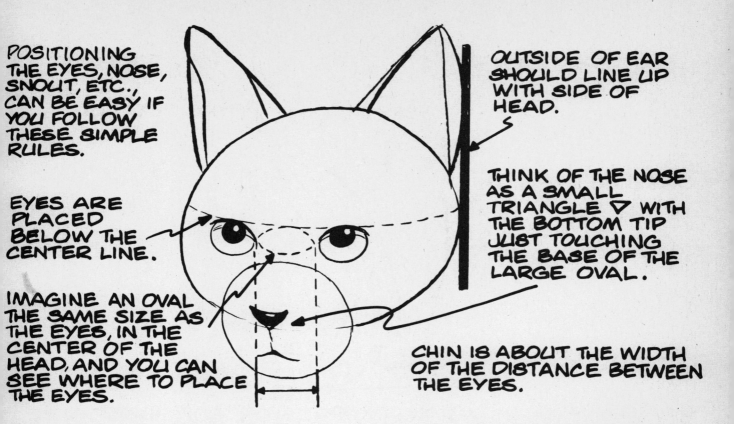

OUTSIDE OF EAR SHOULD LINE UP WITH SIDE OF HEAD.

THINK OF THE NOSE AS A SMALL TRIANGLE ▽ WITH THE BOTTOM TIP JUST TOUCHING THE BASE OF THE LARGE OVAL.

CHIN IS ABOUT THE WIDTH OF THE DISTANCE BETWEEN THE EYES.

HUMAN EYES

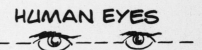

THE SNOUT IS A WEDGE SHAPE.

THE TOP OF THE WEDGE STARTS AT THE CENTER OF EYES AND STOPS AT TOP OF NOSE.

MOUTH, WHEN CLOSED, IS VERY SMALL.

NOTICE THE ANGLE OF THE EYES. HIGHER ON THE OUTSIDE, LOWER ON THE INSIDE.

WEDGE

FRONT VIEW

NOW THE FUN BEGINS. START PUTTING IN THE DETAILS.

HAVE YOU EVER HEARD THE EXPRESSION "BOY, HE RUBS ME THE WRONG WAY"? NOTICE THE DIRECTION OF YOUR CAT'S FUR, WHICH LIES FROM HEAD TO TAIL. CATS DON'T LIKE TO HAVE THEIR FUR RUBBED THE WRONG WAY!

STUDY YOUR CAT AT HOME FOR ALL THESE LITTLE DETAILS.

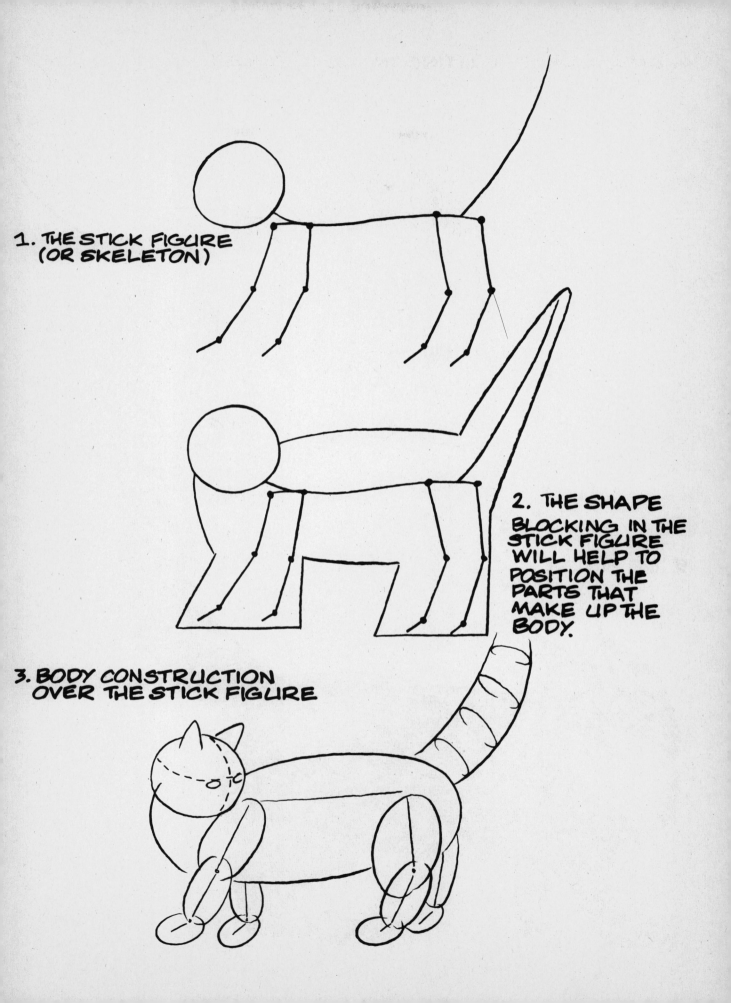

1. THE STICK FIGURE
(OR SKELETON)

2. THE SHAPE
BLOCKING IN THE
STICK FIGURE
WILL HELP TO
POSITION THE
PARTS THAT
MAKE UP THE
BODY.

3. BODY CONSTRUCTION
OVER THE STICK FIGURE

4. CLEAN-UP (OR PUTTING IN THE DETAILS)

5. THE FINISH

HERE'S A CHANCE FOR YOU TO PRACTICE PUTTING IN THE
DETAILS. FINISH THE DRAWING BELOW.

COMPARE THE FINISHED DRAWINGS WITH THE STEP-BY-STEP DRAWINGS. STUDYING THESE DRAWINGS WILL HELP YOU UNDERSTAND THE BASIC CONSTRUCTION AND GIVE YOU A BETTER FINISHED DRAWING.

THE CLEAN-UP

THE FINISH

THE LONG-HAIRED CAT

THE STICK FIGURE

THE OVERALL SHAPE

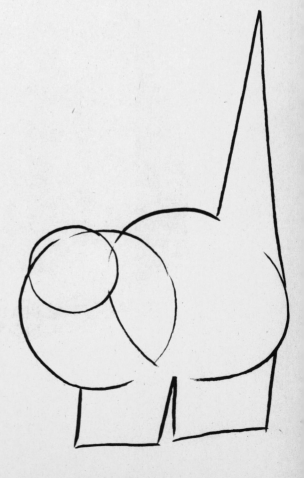

NOTICE HOW FULL THE
LONG-HAIRED CAT BECOMES.

BECAUSE OF ALL THE HAIR
THE FEATURES ARE NOT
AS CLEARLY DEFINED.

THE CLEAN-UP, OR PUTTING IN THE DETAILS

ONCE AGAIN, YOU HAVE TO PAY ATTENTION TO THE FLOW OR DIRECTION OF THE FUR.

THE FINISH

ADULT CAT

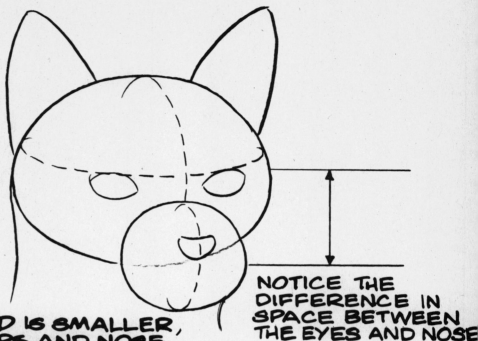

NOTICE THE
DIFFERENCE IN
SPACE BETWEEN
THE EYES AND NOSE

THE KITTEN'S HEAD IS SMALLER,
BUT THE EYES, EARS AND NOSE
DRAWN FAIRLY LARGE WILL
GIVE HER THAT CUTENESS ALL
KITTENS HAVE.

KITTEN

THE SAME BASIC
RULES SUCH AS
CENTER LINES
AND WHERE TO
POSITION FEATURES
APPLY TO THE
KITTEN.

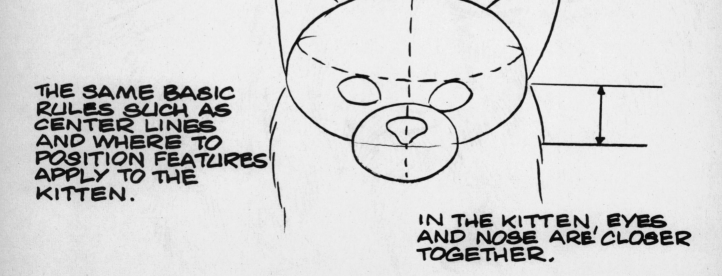

IN THE KITTEN, EYES
AND NOSE ARE CLOSER
TOGETHER.

WHEN DRAWING KITTENS I FIND IT
EASIER TO START WITH THE BASIC
SHAPES AND THEN ADD THE STICK
FIGURE OR SKELETON.

NOTICE HOW SIMPLE
THE CONSTRUCTION
OF KITTENS SEEMS TO BE.

START TO REFINE THE SHAPES.

CENTER LINES

THE FINISH

OVERALL
BASIC SHAPE

ADD SKELETON,
CENTER LINES AND
DEFINITION OF PARTS.

THE CLEAN-UP

THE FINISH

SOME CLOSE-UP DRAWINGS
FOR YOU TO STUDY.

STUDY THE SKETCHES ON THE NEXT FEW PAGES, THEN TRY DOING YOUR OWN.

HERE IS A PRACTICE LESSON TO HELP GIVE YOUR DRAWINGS DEPTH. IT'S EASY... LIGHTLY SKETCH A CIRCLE, OVAL, ETC. AND START DRAWING LOOPS.